The Delights of Reading

The Delights of
READING

Quotes, Notes & Anecdotes

OTTO L. BETTMANN

Foreword by Daniel J. Boorstin

David R. Godine : Publisher : Inc.
in association with
The Center for the Book
in the Library of Congress

First published in 1987 by
David R. Godine, Publisher, Inc.
Horticultural Hall
300 Massachusetts Avenue
Boston, Massachusetts 02115

Acknowledgments

Thanks are due to my indefatigable helpers:
Dianne Skafte, *Literary Consultant*
Greta Larsen, *Coordinator*
George Meyerson, *Bibliographical Research*

Library of Congress Cataloging-in-Publication Data
The Delights of reading.
Includes index.
1. Books and reading—Quotations, maxims, etc.
2. Books and reading—Anecdotes, facetiae, satire, etc.
I. Bettmann, Otto. II. Center for the Book.
Z1003.D34 1987   028'.9'0207   86-46252
ISBN 0-87923-673-6 (HC)
ISBN 0-87923-951-4 (SC)

First softcover printing, 1992
Printed in the United States of America

C O N T E N T S

PART TWO   *The Art of the Pen*

Research
"A man will turn over half a
library to make one book."
Samuel Johnson

Quotesmanship
"By necessity, by proclivity, and
by delight, we all quote."
Ralph Waldo Emerson

.•.

PART THREE *The Literary Establishment*

F O R E W O R D

Daniel J. Boorstin

The Delights of Reading provides us with yet another delightful reason to thank Gutenberg and his successors. For by multiplying the pleasures of reading and by inspiring devotees of the book, they have inspired Otto L. Bettmann to assemble the bounty presented in these pages. There is no greater pleasure than sharing our enthusiasms. As Chesterton once observed, "Enthusiasts soon understand one another"—and what better way to share our enthusiasm than through the medium of the book, what greater joy than introducing a friend to a book we love! And here, with his wonderfully fluent imagination, Otto L. Bettmann offers us the opportunity to share the delight of eloquent, ironic, witty people of all sorts and from all ages.

As the national library of a great free republic, the Library of Congress has a special duty and a special interest to see that books are read and that they are read by people of all ages, races, and social conditions. It is also incumbent on us to insure that books are not buried in their own excess, under their own dross, nor lost from neglect or obscured by specious alternatives and synthetic substitutes. Through its Center for the Book, the Library shapes ambitious plans to make Americans eager, avid, understanding, and critical readers.

We also want to remind Americans of the joys of reading. This book does just that, and does so in abundance. Through this selection of quotations and illustrations we can rejoice together in the good fortune of our heritage and of our opportunities. We see that books are companions always ready to serve, entertain, and inform. We also see that books remind us that we are not alone. As James Baldwin once observed:

> You think your pain and your heartbreak are unprecedented in the history of the world, but then you read. It was books that taught me that the things that tormented me the most were the very things that connected me with all the people who were alive, or who had ever been alive.

This is an unusual book of quotations. It is serious but not solemn. The quotations are arranged into what Dr. Bettmann calls "sense-making categories," within which he has attempted to achieve a logical progression. Pungency of phrase and verbal elegance were his criteria for selection, along with subject matter. Acerbic comments add spice. Careful readers will notice a deliberate circularity, with the beginning themes of each section modulated, fugue-like, until a final statement repeats the theme. The author's hometown of Leipzig, Germany, a center not only of books but also of Bach, the fugal master, undoubtedly provides this subtle and rewarding influence.

Another novel feature is the book's use of images. And could anything be more appropriate, for the author was the founder of the Bettmann Archive in New York, a pictorial resource of national significance. While the Archive covers the whole gamut of human history, the creator of the Archive has always had a predilection for books, printing, and reading.

During the days of the Weimar Republic, Dr. Bettmann was a rare-book librarian at the State Library in Berlin. The arts and literature were flourishing, and he was assigned to assemble an exhibit on "The Book in Art." The display he assembled included miniature paintings of readers, plus woodcuts and engravings of writers and libraries—the whole world of books in graphic array. He was forced to leave his post after Hitler's rise, but the collection he assembled continued to grow in size and scope. Happily, he and his collection relocated in the United States in 1935.

Today Dr. Bettmann lives in Florida and is on the advisory board of the Florida Center for the Book, an affiliate of the Center for the Book in the Library of Congress. His love of words, books, and libraries matches his knowledge of and enthusiasm for graphic illustration. America's libraries, in particular, still amaze him:

> Once as a boy of twelve I was emboldened to search for some books in Leipzig's Municipal Library. To be admitted to its august precincts as a regular user one needed pledges from three citizens of high standing. After securing these I presented my "want list" to the librarian. Like a dragon protecting his holy grail he viewed me critically, then blurted out with the friendliness of a drill sergeant— "come back in three days and we will show you what we have found."
>
> No wonder that, by contrast, I was startled upon my arrival in America to find its libraries groaning with books liberally available to all citizens, with no questions asked. This struck me, accustomed to the lean library diet of the old country, as one of the most remarkable features of American democratic life.

The Center for the Book in the Library of Congress is proud to be associated with this original, graphically arresting, and verbally fetching tribute to the book. May it help us all be A Nation of Readers.

❖

I have laboriously collected this cento out of diverse writers. I have wronged no authors but given every man his own. . . . Bees do little harm and damage no one in extracting honey; I can say of myself, whom have I injured? The matter is theirs most part, and yet mine. . . . it becomes something different in its new setting.

: ROBERT BURTON,
Anatomy of Melancholy

Lincoln reading to his son Tad

PART ONE

Invitation to Reading

Behold a Book . . .

I will nourish with it five thousand souls, a
hundred thousand souls, a million
souls . . . all humanity. . . .
: Victor Hugo

⊶

GUTENBERG IS forever the auxiliary of life; he
is the permanent fellow-workman in the great work
of civilization . . . he has marked the transition of
the man-slave to the free-man. *: Victor Hugo*

⊷

ALL THE glory of the world would be buried in
oblivion, unless God had provided mortals the
remedy of books. *: Richard de Bury*

⊶

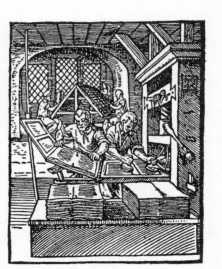

*Printshop of 16th century (Woodcut
by Jost Amman)*

THE PRINTED page illuminates the mind of man
and defies, as far as anything sublimary can, the
corrosive hand of time. *: Denys Hay*

⊷

O PRINTING! How hath thou disturbed the peace
of mankind! That lead when molded into bullets
is not so mortal as when founded into letters.
: Andrew Marvell

*This celestial cornucopia presents
books to an expectant humanity
(Wash drawing by J. Rips, c. 1750)*

Lɪᴋᴇ ᴀɴʏ other extension of man, typography had psychic and social consequences that suddenly shifted previous boundaries and patterns of culture. In bringing the ancient and medieval worlds into fusion—or, as some would say, confusion—the printed book created a third world, the modern world, which now encounters new electric technology or a new extension of man.
: *Marshall McLuhan*

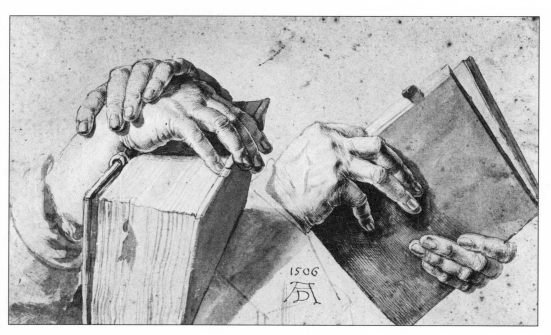

Hands holding books (Charcoal drawing by Albrecht Dürer, 1506)

Gutenberg showing the first sheets
from his press to an early patron.
(Mural painting by Henry V. Poore)

To THE PRESS alone, checkered as it is with abuse, the world is indebted for all the triumphs which have been gained by reason and humanity over error and oppression. : *Thomas Jefferson*

⁙

The Mind-Expanding Potency of Reading

Books—the best antidote against the
marsh-gas of boredom and vacuity.
: *George Steiner*

❧

Eᴍᴘʟᴏʏ ʏᴏᴜʀ time in improving yourself by other
men's writing so that you shall come easily by what
others have labored hard for. *: Socrates*

*Roman savant studying scroll
in library adjoining atrium*

MOST PEOPLE have learned to read to serve a paltry convenience, as they have learned to cipher in order to keep accounts and not be cheated in trade; but of reading as a noble, intellectual exercise they know little or nothing.
: *Henry David Thoreau*

EVERY MAN who knows how to read has it in his power to magnify himself, to multiply the ways in which he exists, to make his life full, significant, and interesting. : *Aldous Huxley*

IN READING, a lonely quiet concert is given to our minds; all our mental faculties will be present in this symphonic exaltation. : *Stéphane Mallarmé*

Stéphane Mallarmé (Etching by Gauguin)

IT IS CHIEFLY through books that we enjoy the intercourse with superior minds. . . . In the best books, great men talk to us, give us their most precious thoughts, and pour their souls into ours. God be thanked for books.
: *William Ellery Channing*

READING IS to the mind what exercise is to the body. It is wholesome and bracing for the mind to have its faculties kept on the stretch.
: *Augustus Hare*

*Elephant visits library for truncated
reading lesson (18th century engraving)*

YOU CAN practice the art of empathy in all the
novels of Jane Austen and it is this daily practice
that we all need, or we will never be good at living,
as without practice we will never be good at playing the piano. *: Fay Weldon*

⁂

BOOKS HAVE to be read (worse luck it takes so
long a time). It is the only way of discovering what
they contain. A few savage tribes eat them, but
reading is the only method of assimilation revealed
to the West. *: E. M. Forster*

Someone said, "The dead writers are remote from us because we know so much more than they did." Precisely, and they are that which we know.
: T. S. Eliot

❖

Books are a refuge, a sort of cloistral refuge, from the vulgarities of the actual world.
: Walter Pater

❖

A truly good book teaches me better than to read it. I must soon lay it down, and commence living on its hint. . . . What I began by reading, I must finish by acting. *: Henry David Thoreau*

❖

He ate and drank the precious words,
His spirit grew robust;
He knew no more that he was poor,
Nor that his frame was dust.
He danced along the dingy days,
And this bequest of wings
Was but a book. What liberty
A loosened spirit brings!
: Emily Dickinson

❖

Henry David Thoreau reading in the Walden woods

Reading to Relax

No entertainment is so cheap as reading,
nor any pleasure so lasting.
: *Lady Mary Wortley Montagu*

MY BOOK hath been so much my pleasure, and bringeth daily to me more pleasure and more, that in respect of it, all pleasure in very deed be but trifles and troubles unto me. : *Roger Ascham*

"Ichabod Crane"

WHAT IS read with delight is commonly retained, because pleasure always secures attention; but the books which are consulted by occasional necessity, and perused with impatience, seldom leave any traces on the mind. . . . Books that you may carry to the fire, and hold readily in your hand are the most useful, after all . . . such books form the mass of general and easy reading.
: *Samuel Johnson*

READING—the best state yet to keep absolute loneliness at bay. : *William Styron*

*Johann Wolfgang von Goethe reading in the
garden of his Weimar habitat*

❧

I‍F THE reader finds pleasure . . . let him continue; if not, let him throw the book away. The
only criterion in the end is pleasure; all the other
arguments are worthless. : *Claude Simon*

YOUR FAMILY sees you as a lazy lump lying on the couch, propping a book up on your stomach, never realizing that you are really in the midst of an African safari that has just been charged by elephants, or in the drawing room of a large English country house interrogating the butler about the body discovered on the Aubusson carpet.

Reading is an escape, an education, a delving into the brain of another human being on such an intimate level that every nuance of thought, every snapping of synapse, every slippery desire of the author is laid open before you like, well, a book. : *Cynthia Heimel*

Reader dozing off (Drawing by Thackeray)

TO ME, detective stories are a great solace, a sort of mental knitting, where it doesn't matter if you drop a stitch. : *Rupert Hart-Davis*

A LARGE, still book is a piece of quietness, succulent and nourishing in a noisy world, which I approach and imbibe with "a sort of greedy enjoyment," as Marcel Proust said of those rooms of his old home whose air was "saturated with the bouquet of silence." : *Holbrook Jackson*

WE SHOULD read to give our souls a chance to luxuriate. : *Henry Miller*

Without Books, History is Silent

Books rule the world, at least those
nations which have a written language.
The others do not count.

: Voltaire

❖

BOOKS ARE the carriers of civilization. Without books, history is silent, literature dumb, science crippled, thought and speculation at a standstill. They are engines of change, windows on the world, "lighthouses" (as a poet said) "erected in the sea of time." *: Barbara W. Tuchman*

A book group from the original edition of Didbin's Bibliomania— *the classic tract on this affliction*

❖

I GO INTO my library and all history rolls before me. I breathe the morning air of the world while the scent of Eden's roses yet linger in it . . . I see the pyramids building; I hear the shouting of the armies of Alexander . . . I sit as in a theatre—the stage is time, the play is the play of the world. *: Alexander Smith*

❖

WE HAVE preserved the Book, and the Book has preserved us. *: David Ben-Gurion*

I T WAS THE Holy Book, and the study of it, that kept the scattered people together. *: Sigmund Freud*

❖

A N AUTHOR may influence the fortunes of the world to as great an extent as a statesman or a warrior. A book may be as great a thing as a battle, and there are systems of Philosophy which have produced as great revolutions as any that have disturbed the social and political existence of our centuries. *: Benjamin Disraeli*

Allegory of the "compleat bookman" (Painting by the Italian symbolist, Giuseppe Arcimboldo, 1527–1593)

Rapid Readers

He has only half learned the art of
reading who has not added to it the more
refined art of skipping and skimming.

: Arthur, Lord Balfour

*Dr. Samuel Johnson had the reputation
of being a speed reader with the
faculty of appraising a book without
needing to read every word of it*

Samuel Johnson :

HE READ, as he did most things, violently; he
had a peculiar facility for seizing at once what was
valuable in any book, without submitting to the
labour of perusing it from the beginning to end.

He got at the substance of a book directly, tearing out the heart of it. At times he kept a book in readiness for when he should finish the other, resembling a dog who holds a bone in his paws in reserve, while he eats something else which has been thrown to him. *: James Boswell*

·ı·

Napoleon Bonaparte :

HE READ so fast that a book lasted him scarcely one hour, and at Saint Helena, a servant was kept busy carrying away armfuls of finished books which only a day before had been brought from the shelves. *: Emil Ludwig*

·ı·

Thomas Wolfe :

HE READ insanely, by the hundreds, the thousands, the ten thousands, yet he had no desire to be bookish; no one could describe this mad assault upon print as scholarly: a ravening appetite in him demanded that he read everything that had ever been written. *: Lawrence C. Powell*

·ı·

THE ART of reading is among other things the art of adopting that pace the author has set. Some books are fast and some are slow, but no book can be understood if it is taken at the wrong speed. *: Mark Van Doren*

Vapid Readers

Books are the best things, well used;
abused, among the worst.
: Ralph Waldo Emerson

Don Quixote in his library

THE READING of bad books is not only . . .
standing still, but going backwards (and he that
has his head filled with wrong notions is much
more at a distance from the truth than he that is
perfectly ignorant). *: John Locke*

TO STUFF our minds with what is simply trivial,
simply curious, or of a low nutritive power, is to
close our minds to what is solid and enlarging, and
spiritually sustaining. *: Frederic Harrison*

READING made Don Quixote a gentleman. Be-
lieving what he read made him mad.
: George Bernard Shaw

*A Parisian gentleman fantasizing in
the grip of the latest novel (Woodcut, c. 1840)*

THE FOOLISHEST book is a kind of leaky boat
on a sea of wisdom; some of the wisdom will get
in anyway. *: Oliver Wendell Holmes*

❖

BAD BOOKS are better than no books at all.
: Marquise de Sévigné

Read . . . *Everywhere, Everywhen*

The time to read is any time: no
apparatus, no appointment of time and
place, is necessary. It is the only art which
can be practised at any hour of the day or
night, whenever the time and inclination
comes, that is your time for reading; in
joy or sorrow, health or illness.

: Holbrook Jackson

WHETHER I am being shaved, or having my hair
cut, whether I am riding on horseback or taking
my meals, I either read myself or get someone to
read to me. *: Francesco Petrarca*

I KNEW A gentleman who was so good a manager
of his time that he would not even lose that small
portion of it which the calls of nature obliged him
to pass in the necessary-house; but gradually went
through all the Latin poets in those moments.
: Lord Chesterfield

*Blinkered reader encounters a horse
similarly accoutred*

A Victorian fantasy: To conquer tedium—reading while washing the dishes

ANOTHER FAMOUS man who made a practice of reading as he walked the highways was Dr. Johnson, and it is recorded that he presented a curious spectacle indeed, for his short-sightedness compelled him to hold the volume close to the nose, and he shuffled along rather than walked, stepping high over shadows and stumbling over sticks and stones. *: Eugene Field*

ALL MY good reading, you might say, was done in the toilet. . . . There are passages of Ulysses which can be read only in the toilet—if one wants to extract the full flavor of their content.
: Henry Miller

OH! FOR a book, and a cosy nook
    And oh! for a quiet hour,
When care and strife and worry of life,
    Have lost their dreaded power,
When you read with zest the very best
    That mind to mind can give,
And quaff your joy without alloy,
    And feel it is good to live.
: Anonymous

A housewife succeeds in killing two birds with one stone

Books—A Boon to Old . . .

The delights of reading impart the vivacity
of youth even to old age.
: *Isaac D'Israeli*

❖

BOOKS RELIEVE me from idleness, rescue me
from company, blunt the edge of my grief. They
are the comfort and solitude of my old age.
: *Michel de Montaigne*

❖

Artist George Cruickshank, aged 78,
happy as a lark among his books

WHEN SIR Robert Walpole was dismissed from
all his employments he retired to Houghton and
walked into the library. Pulling down a book and
holding it some minutes to his eyes, he burst into
tears. "I have led a life of business so long," said
he, "that I have lost my taste for reading; and
now—what shall I do?"
: *The Oxford Book of Literary Anecdotes*

❖

THIS NICE and subtle happiness of reading, this
joy not chilled by age, this polite and unpunished
vice, this selfish, serene life-long intoxication.
: *Logan Pearsall Smith*

❖

*To read and write in a garden was,
to Montaigne, to blend two of man's
greatest delights*

THE ACTIVE scenes are over at my age. I indulge, with all the art I can, my taste for reading. If I would confine it to valuable books, they are almost as rare as valuable men. I must be content with what I can find. The methods may appear low to busy people; but, I forget my infirmities, and attain very desirable ends.
: *Lady Mary Wortley Montagu*

I CANNOT imagine a pleasanter old age than one spent in the not too remote country where I could reread and annotate my favorite books.
: *André Maurois*

I CANNOT think of a greater blessing than to die in one's own bed, without warning or discomfort, on the last page of the new book that we most wanted to read.
: *John Russell*

*Paris bookworm intrigued by find at
bouquinist's stand near Seine river*

*A ghost novel produces a scare in a
young Victorian reader*

. . . and Young

ALICE WAS beginning to get very tired of sitting by her sister on the bank, and of having nothing to do; once or twice she had peeped into the book her sister was reading, but it had no pictures or conversations in it, "and where is the use of a book," thought Alice, "without pictures or conversation?" : *Lewis Carroll*

Studious New England boy
reads by the fire

DEAR LITTLE child, this little book
Is less a primer than a key
To sunder gates where wonders wait
Your "Open Sesame!"
: *Rupert Hughes*

VERY YOUNG children eat their books, literally devouring their contents. This is one reason for the scarcity of first editions of *Alice in Wonderland* and other favorites of the nursery.
: *A. S. W. Rosenbach*

HOW AM I to sing your praise,
Happy chimney corner days,
Sitting safe in nursery nooks,
Reading picture-story books.
: *Robert Louis Stevenson*

Alice's theory of bookmaking
as stated on first page of
Lewis Carroll's Alice in Wonderland

CHILD! Do not throw this book about!
Refrain from the unholy pleasure
Of cutting all the pictures out.
: Hilaire Belloc

⁘

IT WOULD be a good idea if children would write
books for older people, now that everyone is writing for children. *: G. C. Lichtenberg*

⋎

HE IS A writer for the ages—ages four to eight.
: Dorothy Parker

*G**reat Leaders . . . Great Readers*

❖

I WALKE MANIE times . . . into the pleasant fieldes of the Holye Scriptures, where I pluck up the goodlie greene herbes of sentences, eate them by reading, chewe them up musing, and laie them up at length in the seate of memorie . . . so I may the lesse perceive the bitterness of this miserable life.
: *Queen Elizabeth I*

❖

King James I :

WHEN HE came to see our University of Oxford, and went to view that famous library, renewed by Sir Thomas Bodley, at his departure brake out into that noble speech: "If I were not a king, I would be a university man: and if it were so that I must be a prisoner, I would desire to have no other prison than that library . . . and to be chained together with so many good authors."
: *Robert Burton*

Queen Elizabeth, an ardent book collector and Latinist

❖

I WOULD advise you to read with a pen in your hand, and enter in a little book short hints of what you find that is curious, or that might be useful; for this will be the best method of imprinting such particulars in your memory, where they will be ready, on some future occasion, to adorn and improve your conversation. : *Benjamin Franklin*

Abraham Lincoln :

"THE THINGS I want to know are in books. My best friend is the man who will get me a book I ain't read" . . . Since early youth he was possessed by a passion for books and borrowed any he could lay his hands on "in a radius of fifty miles." He kept with him even when working in the field some books to read during periods of rest. . . . When he travelled over the circuit, he often carried with him a volume of Shakespeare to read during spare moments. *: M. L. Houser*

Lincoln reading by light of a fireplace

William Ewart Gladstone in his library. The eminent politician was also an erudite classical scholar

BOOKS ARE delightful society. If you go into a room and find it full of books—even without taking them from the shelves they seem to speak to you, to bid you welcome. They seem to tell you that they have got something inside their covers that will be good for you, and that they are willing and desirous to impart to you. Value them much.
: *William Ewart Gladstone*

Daniel O'Connell :

THIS FAMOUS Irish agitator was travelling with a friend when the November number of *The Old Curiosity Shop* came out. He bought a copy, and as he read it his eyes filled with tears, and he began to sob aloud. "He should not have killed her!—he should not have killed her!—she was too good!" he exclaimed; and in grief and indignation he threw the book out of the window. *: Amy Cruse*

⁂

HARRY TRUMAN was one of our most bookish Presidents. "Ken McCormick of Doubleday re-members going up to see him at the Waldorf-As-toria Hotel after Truman had left the White House. He arrived early in the morning and the President wasn't up yet, but Mrs. Truman said, 'Go right into his bedroom—he'd love to see you, Ken.' So Ken walked in, and there was the President, the former President, sitting in a big chair with two stacks of new books on either side of his chair. Ken said, 'Mr. President, as a publisher, I'm so pleased to see that you're buying all those books. I suppose you read yourself to sleep at night.' He said, 'No, young man, I read myself awake.' "
: David McCullough

⁂

WHEN the town of Franklin, Massachusetts, asked Franklin to donate funds toward the purchase of a bell for the meeting-house chapel, he advised that he would donate books instead, "Sense being preferable to sound." *: John Clyde Oswald*

Books of Our Own

Build yourself a book-nest to forget the
world without.
: *Abraham Cowley*

⁙

A ROOM without books is a body without a soul.
: *Marcus Tullius Cicero*

⁙

KNOWING I lov'd my books, he furnished me
from mine own library with volumes that I prize
above a dukedom. : *William Shakespeare*

⁙

A LIBRARY OF wisdom, is more precious than
all wealth, and all things that are desirable cannot
be compared to it. Whoever therefore claims to
be zealous of truth, of happiness, of wisdom or
knowledge, aye even of the faith, must needs become a lover of books. : *Richard de Bury*

Intense nocturnal study

⁙

I NO SOONER come into the library, but I bolt
the door, excluding lust, ambition, avarice . . . in
the lap of eternity amongst so many divine souls,
I take my seat with so lofty a spirit and sweet
content that I pity all our great ones and rich men
who know not this happiness. : *Robert Burton*

*A nobleman of the rococo period
proudly supervises work on his
wall-to-wall leatherbound treasures*

A BOOK READS the better, which is our own, and has been so long known to us, that we know the topography of its blots, and dog's ears, and can trace the dirt in it to having read it at tea with buttered muffins. : *Charles Lamb*

Ralph Waldo Emerson

CONSIDER what you have in the smallest chosen library: a company of the wisest and wittiest men that could be picked out of all civil countries in a thousand years. . . . The thought which they did not uncover to their bosom friend is here written out in transparent words to us, the strangers of another age. : *Ralph Waldo Emerson*

No FURNITURE is so charming as books. . . .
Even if you never open them, or read a single
word; the plainest row of cloth or paper covered
books is more significant of refinement than the
most elaborately carved étagère or sideboard.
: *Sydney Smith*

WHEN SIR Walter Scott returned to Abbotsford
to die and was wheeled into his library, he burst
into tears as he beheld those lifelong friends upon
his bookshelves.
: *The Oxford Book of Literary Anecdotes*

I HAVE ALWAYS loved the idea of those pious
Jews who envisaged the world to come: as an
immense library, where all the truly good books
written by man would be available to the righteous
dead. : *Leo Rosten*

A GOOD BOOK is always on tap; it may be de-
canted and drunk a hundred times, and it is still
there for further imbibement.
: *Holbrook Jackson*

The Bookworm (Painting by the German genre painter Carl Spitzweg, 1808–1878)

Books for All: Public Libraries

Places of sanctuary for individuality, singularity, and the right of man to make up his own mind.

: Frances Clarke Sayers

*Books for the few: A Dutch scholar
consults a chained book in library
of University of Leyden*

A LIBRARY IS that venerable place where men preserve the history of their experience, their tentative experiments, their discoveries, and their plans . . . in books may be found the recipes for daily living—the prescriptions for the mind and the heart. *: Georges Duhamel*

A LIBRARY IS the delivery room for the birth of ideas, a place where history comes to life.
: *Norman Cousins*

THEY ARE concert halls of the finest voices, where men, properly informed, might bring forth something for ornament, much for curiosity, and more for use. : *Henry Ward Beecher*

INSTEAD OF going to Paris to attend lectures, go to the public library, and you won't come out for twenty years, if you really wish to learn.
: *Leo Tolstoy*

THE TIME *was* when a library was very like a museum and the librarian was a mouser in musty books. The time *is* when the library is a school and the librarian is in the highest sense a teacher, and a reader is a workman among his tools.
: *Melvil Dewey*

A lending library for the young near St. Paul's, London

SINCE MY family did not own many books or have the money for a child to buy them, it was good to know that solely by virtue of my municipal citizenship I had access to any book I wanted . . . from the branch library I could walk to in my neighborhood. : *Philip Roth*

THE BEST of my education has come from the public library . . . my tuition fee is a bus fare and once in a while, five cents a day for an overdue book. You don't need to know very much to start with, if you know the way to the public library.
: *Lesley Conger*

*The antidust safety helmet suggested
for librarians of the old school*

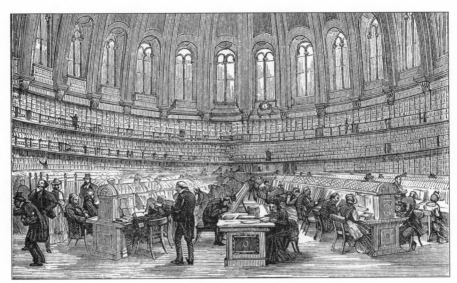

The reading room of the British Museum

Three Giants of Bookdom

I F TRUTH is not to be found in the British Museum . . . where is truth? *: Virginia Woolf*

·▪·

T HE NEW YORK Public Library's large, easy-going, generous—like New York itself. *: Marchette Chute*

▪

T HE LIBRARY of Congress, taking all knowledge for its province, is a symbol of a free people and its government. *: Daniel J. Boorstin*

IN NO OTHER country of the world is the nation so much and systematically instructed outside the school as in America . . . one more lively testimony to the tireless instinct for personal perfection. The background of all of this is the great national stock of public library books. Even the poorest person can study them in the most delightful surroundings. *: Hugo Münsterberg*

∴

WHEN A don asked me how many books I had I really couldn't reply, but this didn't matter. I was too polite to deliver a variant of Samuel Butler's "I keep my books around the corner, in the British Museum." *: Philip Larkin*

Andrew Carnegie munificently endowed library building in the United States

*L*enders Beware!

Everything comes to him who waits,
except a loaned book.
: McKinney Hubbard

GREAT COLLECTIONS of books are subject to certain accidents besides the damp, the worms, and the rats; one not less common is that of the borrowers, not to say a word of the purloiners. *: Isaac D'Israeli*

STEAL NOT this book, my honest friend,
For fear the gallows should be your end,
And when you die the Lord will say,
And ware's the book you stole away?
: Richard Hooker

THE OWNER of a country house was showing some visitors his superb library. "Do you ever lend books?" he was asked. "No," he replied promptly, "only fools lend books." Then, waving his hand to a many shelved section filled with handsomely bound volumes, he added, "All those books once belonged to fools." *: Holbrook Jackson*

PLEASE RETURN this book; I find that though many of my friends are poor arithmeticians, they are nearly all good book-keepers. *: Sir Walter Scott*

Anatole France (Pen and ink portrait)

NEVER LEND books, for no one ever returns them; the only books I have in my library are books that other fools have lent me. *: Anatole France*

MUCH HAVE I sorrowed
Learning to my cost
That a book that's borrowed
Is a book that's lost.
: Arthur Guiterman

OFTEN I sat up in my room reading the greatest part of the night, when the book was borrowed in the evening and to be returned early in the morning, lest it should be missed or wanted."
: Benjamin Franklin

Aberrant Booklove:
Bibliomania and Book Gluttony

A bibliomaniac is one to whom books are
like bottles of whiskey to the inebriate, to
whom anything that is between covers has
an intoxicating savor.

: Sir Hugh Walpole

*Isaac Gosse, a ravenous English
book collector*

THE MIND nauseates at the thought of proces-
sions of learned dunces and dullards: . . . popes
of knowledge, wise fools, tyrants of information
who are crammed full of learning but lifeless, stupid, repellent; men who have piled such a load of
books on their heads that their brains have seemed
squashed by them. *: Michel de Montaigne*

An incurable bibliomaniac
(Woodcut by J. J. Grandville)

THE FRENCH collector Boulard was known as one of the most frantic bibliomaniacs who ever lived. He bought books by the yard, by the acre, by the heap, by the basket, retail and wholesale, filling drawing-room, vestibules, lumber-rooms, stairs, bedrooms, and cupboards with them until his house bent under the weight. He collected some 600,000 volumes, which he stored in six houses, evicting the tenants as his hoard grew.
: *Octave Uzanne*

❖

ARCHDEACON MEADOW accumulated so many books that he was forced to sell a considerable portion of his collection. But as their auction proceeded he experienced such passionate anguish that he left the room and returned in disguise to begin bidding for his own books.

❖

ISAAC GOSSET, English bibliomaniac, was said to have risen from his death bed when he was presented with a rare volume which he had long craved.
: *Alan G. Thomas*

❖

I HAVE SEEN men hazard their fortunes, go on long journeys halfway around the world, forge friendships, even lie, cheat and steal, all for the gain of a book. : *A. S. W. Rosenbach*

❖

"Long past bed-time." Enraged wife
scorns her book-addicted husband

Book Lovers Lament: So Little Time to Read

The multitude of books is making us ignorant.

: Voltaire

❖

THE FLOOD of print has turned reading into a process of gulping rather than savoring.
: Warren Chappell

❖

TO BUY books would be a good thing if we also could buy the time to read them. As it is, the act of purchasing them is often mistaken for the assimilation and mastering of their content.
: Arthur Schopenhauer

❖

THE ENORMOUS multiplication of books in every branch of knowledge is one of the greatest evils of this age, since it presents one of the most serious obstacles to the acquisition of correct information by throwing in the reader's way piles of lumber in which he must painfully grope for the scraps of useful matter, peradventure interspersed.
: Edgar Allan Poe

❖

Ramelli's rotating reading machine

WHAT REFUGE is there for the victim who is possessed with the feeling that there are a thousand new books he ought to read, while life is only long enough for him to attempt to read a hundred. *: Oliver Wendell Holmes*

⁘

WHEN A certain French classic was being mentioned—one of the finest novels in the world—Zola said that he had not read it. Somebody said, "But look here, Zola, you really ought to read it." "Read it!" Zola retorted. "One has no time to read!" *: Arnold Bennett*

⁘

OUR JOURNALISM forces us to take an interest in some fresh triviality every day, whereas only three or four books in a lifetime give us anything that is of importance. *: Marcel Proust*

⁘

THE FACULTY of attention has utterly vanished from the Anglo-Saxon mind, extinguished at its source by the big bayadère of journalism, of the newspaper and the picture magazine which keeps screaming, "Look at me." Illustrations, loud simplifications . . . bill poster advertising—only these stand a chance. *: Henry James*

⁘

SCIENCE advances from discovery to discovery. Readers are so busy keeping up that there is a real danger that being well-informed is incompatible with being cultivated. *: Aldous Huxley*

WHERE SHALL we find the time and peace of mind to read the classics, overwhelmed as we are by the avalanche of current events? *: Italo Calvino*

WE ARE doing our reading on the run, snatching time pledged elsewhere. *: Jerome Weidman*

THE READING-machine always wound up and going,
He mastered what was not worth knowing.
: James Russell Lowell

EVEN WHEN reading is impossible, the presence of books acquired (by passionate devotion to them) produces such an ecstasy that the buying of more books than one can peradventure read is nothing less than the soul reaching towards infinity . . . we cherish books even if unread, their mere presence exudes comfort, their ready access, reassurance.
: A. E. Newton

*Lytton Strachey—the paragon of
debunking biographers (Lithograph
from* Vanity Fair)

The Art of the Pen

The Mystique of Authorship

When once the itch of literature has
come over a man, nothing will cure it but
the scratching of a pen.

: Sam Lower

⸙

"How should you like to grow up a clever man and write books?" Oliver considered a little while. . . . "Well well," said the old gentleman, "Don't be afraid! We won't make an author of you while there is an honest trade to be learned, or brickmaking to turn to." *: Charles Dickens*

⸙

Who wants to become a writer? And why? Because it's the answer to everything. It's the steaming reason for living. To note, to pin down, to build up, to be astonished at nothing, to cherish the oddities, to let nothing go down the drain, to make something, to make a great flower out of life, even if it's only a cactus. *: Enid Bagnold*

⸙

My passion was for the pen, the ecstasy of watching my scrawl cover the pages. It is the sort of trance saints speak of—a blissful heightened state in which you at once feel utterly alone and in harmony with the universe. *: Erica Jong*

*Jonathan Odell, loyalist poet of the
American Revolution*

A writer in the process of creation, demonstrating the saying of John Slade; "The hand supports the thought; the abstract battle is concretely fought." (Nabokov)

I AM CONVINCED more and more, day by day, that fine writing is next to fine doing, the top thing in the world. : *John Keats*

How vain it is to sit down to write when you have not stood up to live. : *Henry David Thoreau*

Dancing in all its forms cannot be excluded from the curriculum of all noble education; dancing with the feet, with ideas, with words, and, need I add that one must also be able to dance with the pen? : *Friedrich Nietzsche*

Writing is both mask and unveiling. : *E. B. White*

In a very real sense, the writer writes in order to teach himself; to understand himself, to satisfy himself; the publishing of his ideas, though it brings gratifications, is a curious anticlimax. : *Alfred Kazin*

WHY I WRITE . . . sheer egotism. Desire to seem clever, to be talked about, to be remembered after death, to get your own back on grown-ups who snubbed you in childhood. *: George Orwell*

⁙

I DO THINK that the quality which makes a man want to write and be read is essentially a desire for self-exposure and is masochistic. Like one of those guys who has a compulsion to take his thing out and show it on the street. *: James Jones*

⁙

I WRITE IN order to attain that feeling of tension relieved and function achieved which a cow enjoys on giving milk. *: H. L. Mencken*

⁙

THE ART OF writing is the art of applying the seat of the pants to the seat of the chair.
: Mary Heaton Vorse

⁙

The Writer's Life

~~~~~~

A BLEND OF ECSTASY AND TORMENT

Writing is a dog's life, but the only life worth living.
: *Gustave Flaubert*

❖

I HAVE NEVER found, in anything outside of the four walls of my study, an enjoyment equal to sitting at my writing desk with a clean page, a new theme, and a mind awake. : *Washington Irving*

❖

HENRY JAMES joyously engaged in the act of writing. A good day's writing gave him a sense of strength, of control over chaos, a victory of order and clarity over the confused battle of existence. : *Leon Edel*

❖

I SHALL LIVE bad if I do not write, and I shall write bad if I do not live. : *Françoise Sagan*

❖

WHAT A BITCH of a thing prose is! It is never finished; there is always something to be done over . . . Bovary is alien to me. Writing this book, I am like a man playing the piano with lead balls attached to his knuckles. *: Gustave Flaubert*

WRITING IS utter solitude, the descent into the cold abyss of oneself. *: Franz Kafka*

ONE OUGHT only to write when one leaves a piece of one's own flesh in the inkpot, each time one dips one's pen. *: Leo Tolstoy*

EVERY DAY I begin my work with the same odd feeling, that I am on trial for my life and will probably not be acquitted. *: Van Wyck Brooks*

The Utopian view of writing: Let literary alembic congeal existing elements and deliver a perfect masterwork

WHAT THINGS there are to write, if one could only write them! My mind is full of gleaming thought; gay moods and mysterious, moth-like meditations hover in my imagination, fanning their painted wings. But always the rarest, those streaked with azure and the deepest crimson, flutter away beyond my reach. *: Logan Pearsall Smith*

Mark Twain "sweating it out,"
demonstrating the old saw that a
waste-paper bin is a writer's best friend

❖

THE ARTIST'S only responsibility is to his art. He
will be completely ruthless if he is a good one. . . . If
a writer has to rob his mother, he will not hesitate;
the *Ode on a Grecian Urn* is worth any number
of old ladies. *: William Faulkner*

SINCE I began [writing] I have been called off at least a dozen times; once for the fish-man, once by a man who had brought me apples, once to see a book agent, then to make a chowder . . . and now I am at it again, for nothing but deadly determination ever enables me to write. It is rowing against wind and tide. *: Harriet Beecher Stowe*

WRITING A book is a horrible, exhausting struggle, like a long bout of some painful illness. One would never undertake such a thing if one were not driven on by some demon whom one can neither resist nor understand. *: Winston Churchill*

*Obsessive writer's continuous output
dissected by literary cook*

I DO NOT like to write—I like to have written.
: *Gloria Steinem*

Joseph Conrad :

HE ALMOST needed a Caesarean of the soul before he was delivered of his masterwork.
: *Jeffrey Berman*

Mark Twain :

"THERE AIN'T nothing more to write about, and I am rotten glad of it, because if I'd a'knowed what a trouble it was to make a book I wouldn't a'tackled it, and ain't a'going to no more."

Stephen Vincent Benét :

WHEN ASKED how it felt to write "John Brown's Body," he answered, "Just about like giving birth to a grand piano."

The Power of Words

> The art of the pen is to rouse the inward
> vision, to spring imagination with a word or a phrase.
> *: George Meredith*

❖

No IRON can pierce the heart with the force of a well-placed phrase. *: Isaac Babel*

❖

But WORDS are things, and a small drop of ink,
Falling like dew, upon a thought, produces
That which, makes thousands, perhaps millions,
  think. *: Lord Byron*

❖

How EASILY the great men achieve their effects by means extraneous to art. What is more badly put together than much of Rabelais, Cervantes, Molière, and Hugo? But such quick punches! Such power in a single word. We have to pile up a lot of little pebbles to build our pyramids; theirs, a hundred times greater, are made with a single block. *: Gustave Flaubert*

Robert Louis Stevenson

Bright is the ring of words when the right man rings them. *: Robert Louis Stevenson*

However much we may admire the orator's burst of eloquence, the noblest written words are as far above the fleeting spoken language as the firmament with its stars is behind the clouds.
: Henry David Thoreau

One must be drenched in words, literally soaked in them, to have the right ones form themselves into the proper pattern at the right moment.
: Hart Crane

IT IS NOT pathetic passages that make us shed our best tears, but the miracle of a word in the right place. *: Jean Cocteau*

HE THAT uses many words for the explaining any subject doth, like the cuttlefish, hide himself for the most part in his own ink. *: John Ray*

USE WORDS that soak up life. *: Virginia Woolf*

Gustave Flaubert's great novels were born in an atmosphere of agonizing self-criticism

MY TASK, which I am trying to achieve, is, by the power of the written word, to make you hear, to make you feel—it is, before all, to make you see. *: Joseph Conrad*

IF YOU LOOK after them you can build bridges across incomprehension and chaos. They deserve respect. If you get the right ones in the right order, you can nudge the world a little or make a poem which children will speak for you when you are dead. *: Tom Stoppard*

SOME SAY that nothing is more vivid or memorable than a picture. We disagree. No visual image is as vivid as the image created by the mind in response to words. There is more to life than meets the eye. The ability of words to throw a loop around human personality and penetrate the inner space of character is exceeded by nothing that can be given visual form. : *Norman Cousins*

THE WORD persists; the word, spoken or unspoken, frames every feeling, every new thought, wrenched or reclaimed from the universal matrix, chaos. : *Sir Osbert Sitwell*

Literary Genres

A novel is a garden carried in the pocket.
: Arabian proverb

❖

A GOOD NOVEL tells us the truth about its hero; but a bad novel tells us the truth about its author. *: G. K. Chesterton*

❖

THE NOVEL can make the whole man tremble . . . which is more than any other book-tremulation can do. *: D. H. Lawrence*

❖

A GREAT WRITER creates a world of his own, and readers are proud to live in it. A lesser writer may entice them in for a moment, but soon he will watch them filing out. *: Cyril Connolly*

❖

AN INTERVIEWER asked me what book I thought best represented the modern American woman. All I could think of to answer was: *Madame Bovary. : Mary McCarthy*

Illustration from Madame Bovary

NOVELISTS . . . fashioning nets to sustain and support the reader as he falls helplessly through the chaos of his own existence. *: Fay Weldon*

❖

BIOGRAPHY/HISTORY

READ NO history; nothing but biography; for that is life without theory. *: Benjamin Disraeli*

❖

A WELL WRITTEN life is almost as rare as a well-spent one. *: Thomas Carlyle*

BIOGRAPHY . . . performs for us some of the work of fiction, reminding us, that is, of the truly mangled tissue of man's nature and how huge faults and virtues cohabit and persevere in the same character. *: Robert Louis Stevenson*

THE READER wants super highways, he is in a hurry . . . clutter merely clots the story. Did the hero consistently undertip the waitresses? He doesn't want to hear about it . . . nor the heroine's curious breakfast habits, or the hero's theories about shoe lacing. *: John E. O'Hara*

TO PRESERVE a becoming brevity, a brevity which excludes everything that is redundant and nothing that is significant, that surely is the first duty of the biographer. *: Lytton Strachey*

The poet's sleepless night, from a 17th century tract on poetry

POETRY

THE CROWN of literature is poetry. . . . The writer of prose can only step aside when the poet passes. *: W. Somerset Maugham*

WHILE PENSIVE poets painful vigils keep
Sleepless themselves they give their readers sleep.
: Alexander Pope

WHO IS this Pope that I hear so much about? I cannot discover what is his merit. Why will not my subjects write in prose? I hear a great deal, too, of Shakespeare, but I cannot read him, he is such a bombast fellow. *: King George II*

POETS AND pastry cooks will be the same
Since both of them their images must frame.
Chimeras from the poet's fancy flow,
The cook contrives his shapes in real dough.
: William King

POETS ARE the trumpets that sing to battle; poets are the unacknowledged legislators of the world.
: Percy Bysshe Shelley

PUBLISHING a volume of verse is like dropping a rose petal down the Grand Canyon and waiting for the echo. *: Don Marquis*

THERE IS no frigate like a book
To take us lands away,
Nor any coursers like a page
Of prancing poetry.
: Emily Dickinson

A POEM IS never finished—only abandoned.
: *Paul Valéry*

⁂

THE THEATER

THEATRE ADDS to living by being more than life.
: *John Mason Brown*

⁂

GENERALLY speaking, the theatre is the literature of society people who have no time to read.
: *Charles Sainte-Beuve*

⁂

NOT TO GO to the theatre is like making one's
toilet without a mirror. : *Arthur Schopenhauer*

⁂

DRAMA, INSTEAD of telling us the whole of a
man's life, must place him in such a situation, tie
such a knot, that when it is untied, the whole man
is visible. : *Leo Tolstoy*

⁂

SHAKESPEARE frightens me the more I think of
him. In their entirety, I find his works stupendous,
exalting, like the idea of the planetary system. I
only see an immensity there, dazzling and bewil-
dering to the eye. : *Gustave Flaubert*

*This Shadowe is renowned Shakespear's Soule of th'age
The applause? delight? the wonder of the Stage.
Nature her selfe, was proud of his designes
And joy'd to weare the dressing of his lines,
The learned will Confess, his works are such,
As neither man, nor Muse, can prayse to much.
For ever live thy fame, the world to tell,
Thy like, no age, shall ever paralell.
W.M. sculpsit.*

Shakespeare

⁂ 69 ⁑

The Writer's Resources

Talent alone cannot make a writer; there
must be a man behind the book.
: *Ralph Waldo Emerson*

❖

FIND OUT the reason that commands you to write;
see whether it has spread its roots into the very
depth of your heart; confess to yourself you would
have to die if you were forbidden to write.
: *Rainer Maria Rilke*

❖

BOOKS WANT to be born: I never make them.
They come to me and insist on being written, and
on being such and such. : *Samuel Butler*

❖

IT TOOK ME fifteen years to discover I had no
talent for writing, but I couldn't give it up because
by that time I was too famous. : *Robert Benchley*

❖

A MAN WILL turn over half a library to make one book. *: Samuel Johnson*

⁂

WE ENRICH ourselves by discovering and rediscovering our great books—and then writing better books that reach more people, more deeply and more permanently. *: Daniel J. Boorstin*

Stoic female researcher prepares to tackle a giant tome; oversized books were the nemesis of old school librarians (Woodcut, c. 1870)

WRITERS OUGHT not to look with awe upon libraries, as if libraries were Greek temples or holy shrines. Libraries must always be lumberyards to us, houses of building supplies. We go there for the facts, dates, documentation that are the cinderblocks and cellar beams of our work.
: *James Kilpatrick*

◆

QUOTESMANSHIP AND ITS LIMITS

BY NECESSITY, by proclivity, and by delight, we all quote. : *Ralph Waldo Emerson*

◆

IT'S SUCH a pleasure to write down splendid words—almost as though one were inventing them.
: *Rupert Hart-Davis*

◆

ONE ADVANTAGE there certainly is in quotation, that if the authors cited be good, there is at least so much worth reading in the book of him who quotes them. : *Samuel Johnson*

◆

YOU HAVE to read in order to write . . . art is a seamless web, and we all latch into it where we find a loose end. : *Archibald MacLeish*

◆

Dr. Samuel Johnson

FINE WORDS —I wonder where you stole them.
: *Jonathan Swift*

WELL stolen is half written.
: *Arnold Schoenberg*

IF WE STEAL thoughts from the moderns, it will
be cried down as plagiarism; if from the ancients,
it will be cried up as erudition.
: *Charles Caleb Colton*

YOUR COMEDY I've read, my friend,
And like the half you pilfered best;
Be sure the piece you yet may mend—
Take courage, man, and steal the rest.
: *Anonymous*

Writers as Readers

Writers generally enjoy reading, just as
readers feel they might have been writers.
: *Holbrook Jackson*

❧

*Joseph Conrad reading (Sketch by
Sir William Rothenstein)*

Montaigne :

HE WAS NOT a regular, laborious reader, but
loved to sup here and sample there, to roam and
browse and chew the cud. He frankly admitted a
preference even for desultory and idle reading which
so many were apt to condemn, but which had its
place with him. : *Holbrook Jackson*

Percy Bysshe Shelley :

Hᴇ ᴡᴀꜱ ᴀʟᴡᴀʏꜱ reading. At his meals an open book lay by his side on the table. His mutton and potatoes might grow cold, but his interest in a work never cooled. He invariably sallied forth, book in hand, reading to himself if alone, or aloud if he had a companion. He took a volume to bed with him and read as long as his candle lasted; then he slept—impatiently, no doubt—until it was light, and he recommenced reading at the early dawn. : *Thomas Jefferson Hogg*

*Tolstoy reading by candlelight
(Sketched by friend, Ilya Repin)*

Iʟ ʟᴏᴠᴇ ᴛᴏ lose myself in other men's minds. When I am not walking, I am reading; books think for me. : *Charles Lamb*

George Eliot:

Sʜᴇ ᴄᴏɴꜰᴇꜱꜱᴇᴅ that Rousseau's genius sent an electric thrill through her intellectual and moral frame, awakening new perceptions and making man and nature a world of freed thought and feeling, not by his teaching, but by the rushing mighty wind of his inspiration.

Tʜʀᴇᴇ ᴛɪᴍᴇꜱ in my life I have read through Shakespeare and Goethe from end to end. And I never could make out in which their charm consisted. : *Leo Tolstoy*

Books BORED me to death. I am disgusted with all that; only Victor Hugo's theatre and poetry and a book by Sainte-Beuve [*Volupté*] gave me any pleasure. I am absolutely fed up with literature. *: Charles Baudelaire*

Keep AWAY from books; and from men who get their ideas from books, and your own books will always be fresh. *: George Bernard Shaw*

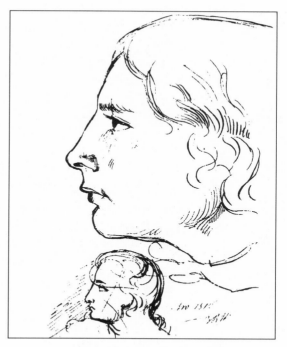

John Keats, sketched by Benjamin Robert Haydon, 1816

G. K. Chesterton:

CHESTERTON was once asked what books he would most like to have with him if he were stranded on a desert island. *"Thomas's Guide to Practical Shipbuilding,"* he replied.

Willa Cather:

HER EYE, her ear, were tuning-forks, burning-glasses, which caught the minutest refraction or echo of a thought or feeling. . . . She heard a deeper vibration, a kind of composite echo, of all that the writer said, and did not say.

Mark Twain:

ASKED WHETHER he liked books, Mark Twain said that he liked a thin book because it would steady a table, a leather volume because it would strop a razor, and a heavy book because it could be thrown at a cat.

Advice and Solace from the Masters

If a book come from the heart, it will contrive to reach other hearts.
: *Thomas Carlyle*

❖

TO WRITE well, express yourself like the common people, but think like a wise man. : *Aristotle*

❖

NO MAN should ever publish a book until he has first read it to a woman. : *Van Wyck Brooks*

❖

FORGET NOT that you write for the stupid—that is, that your maximum of refinement must meet the minimum of intelligence of the audience, in other words the biggest ass it may conceivably contain. : *Henry James*

Henry James, aristocrat to the core, advised "to write for the stupid"

❖

A GOOD NOVEL cannot be too long nor a bad novel too short. : *Ellen Glasgow*

Franz Kafka—reading to torment the soul

THE MOST essential gift for a good writer is a built-in shockproof shit-detector.
: *Ernest Hemingway*

DEAR AUTHOR! Suit your topics to your strength And ponder well your subject and its length.
: *Lord Byron*

THE TWO most engaging powers of an author are to make new things familiar and familiar things new. : *Samuel Johnson*

A BOOK MUST be an ice-axe to break the seas frozen inside our soul. : *Franz Kafka*

WHENEVER I find myself growing vaporish, I rouse myself, wash and put on a clean shirt, brush my hair and clothes, tie my shoestrings neatly, and in fact adozine as if I were going out—then, all clean and comfortable I sit down to write.
: *John Keats*

THE BEST style is the style you don't notice.
: *Somerset Maugham*

⁙

TO PRODUCE a mighty book, you must choose a mighty theme. No great and enduring volume can ever be written on the flea, though many there be that have tried it. : *Herman Melville*

⁙

THAT LAST thing one discovers in writing a book is what to put first. : *Blaise Pascal*

⁙

IN DEPICTING "the motions of the human heart," the durability of the writing depends upon its ex-actitude. It is the thing that is true and stays true for the new reader. : *Ezra Pound*

⁙

YOU WRITE with ease, to show your breeding, But easy writing's vile hard reading.
: *Richard Brinsley Sheridan*

⁙

THERE ARE thousands of thoughts lying within a man that he does not know till he takes up the pen and writes. : *William Makepeace Thackeray*

Ezra Pound: "The durability of writing depends on its exactitude."

THE MOST important thing in a work of art is that it should have some kind of focus . . . there should be some place where all the rays meet, or from which they issue. : *Leo Tolstoy*

WRITE WITHOUT pay until somebody offers pay. If nobody offers within three years, the candidate may look upon this as the sign that sawing wood is what he was intended for. : *Mark Twain*

NO BOOK is born entire and uncrippled as it was conceived. : *Virginia Woolf*

O*mnia quae scripsi paleae mihi videntur.* (All I have written seems to me chaff.)
: *Thomas Aquinas*

Starving author pleads with plump
publisher

The Literary Establishment

*P*ublishers and Authors:
A Friendly Tug of War

⁂

IN SPITE of good will, and frequently of true friendship, author and publisher are natural Antagonists. . . . Authors, as everybody knows, are difficult; they are unreliable, arrogant, and grasping. But publishers are impossible—grasping, arrogant, and unreliable. *: Jacques Barzun*

THE LAND of literature is a fairyland to those who view it at a distance, but, like all other landscapes, the charm fades on nearer approach, and the thorns and briars become visible. The republic of letters is the most factious and discordant of all republics, ancient or modern. *: Washington Irving*

PUBLISHERS ARE a band of panderers which sprung into existence soon after the death of Gutenberg and which now overrun the world. *: Elbert Hubbard*

PUBLISHERS ARE cohorts of the devil: there must be a special hell preserved for them. *: Johann Wolfgang von Goethe*

I STILL MAINTAIN that the publishers of our country are as niggardly a set as ever snapped fingers at a poor devil author.
: *Henry Wadsworth Longfellow*

☙

WE ALWAYS find a lurking reproach that publishers exploit the intellectual work of their authors—that they "drink champagne from bowls made out of the skulls of authors who have been slowly starved to death." : *Siegfried Unseld*

*Your manuscript is both good and original—
but the part that is good is not original and
the part that is original is not good
(Samuel Johnson)*

MY THANKS are due . . . to my Publishers for
their aid, their tact, their energy, their practical
sense, and frank liberality they have afforded an
unknown and unrecommended author.
: *Charlotte Brontë*

❦

WHEN I BEGAN to write, publishers were gentle-
men in tweed jackets puffing pipes. Now . . . publishing houses are owned by oil compa-
nies . . . and their interest is naturally in the big
strike, the gusher. . . . I don't want to write a
gusher. . . . I want to write books that unlock the
traffic jam in everybody's head. : *John Updike*

❖

WHEN HORACE Liveright sold Dreiser's *American Tragedy* to the movies, Dreiser got into an
argument with the publisher during a luncheon at
the Ritz Hotel in New York. At the height of the
altercation, as Bennett Cerf recalls, the waiter
served the coffee. Suddenly Dreiser seized the cup
and threw it in Liveright's face. Horace jumped
up, coffee streaming down his shirt front. Dreiser
got up from the table without a word and marched
out of the restaurant. Horace, always the show-
man, stood there mopping himself up and retained
enough of his equilibrium to say, "Bennett, let
this be a lesson to you. Every author is a son of
a bitch." : *Bennett Cerf*

❦

Writing: A Scant Sustenance

The profession of book writing makes
horse racing seem like a solid, stable business.
: John Steinbeck

⁂

IS NOT A patron, my Lord, one who looks with
unconcern on a man struggling for life in the water,
and, when he has reached the ground, encumbers
him with help? The notice which you have been
pleased to take of my labours, had it been early,
had been kind; but it has been delayed till I am
indifferent, and cannot enjoy it; till I am solitary,
and cannot impart it; till I am known, and do not
want it. *: Samuel Johnson to the Right Honourable
The Earl of Chesterfield: February 7, 1755*

❖

Henry David Thoreau :

IN EARLY 1859, Thoreau sent a contribution of
five dollars to the Harvard Library and noted: "I
would gladly give more, but this exceeds my income from all sources together for the last four
months." He offered his books to Harper's, but
found "they are making fifty thousand dollars an-
nually . . . and their motto is to let well enough
alone . . ." In 1853, Thoreau discovered that his
A Week on the Concord and Merrimack Rivers had

*Walden. This perpetual international
best-seller (it is very popular in
Russia) brought Thoreau but a
pittance of an income*

sold only 219 copies since its publication in 1849. When his publisher returned the remainder, Thoreau wryly mused, "I have now a library of nearly nine hundred volumes, over seven hundred of which I wrote myself." *: Philip Van Doren Stern*

INDEED, AS regards remuneration for the time to write the novel [*The Warden*]—stonebreaking would have done better. *: Anthony Trollope*

I HEREBY GIVE notice that I shall strike for wages . . . I won't work under prices . . . I am a better workman than most in your crew and deserve a better price. You must not, I repeat, be angry or because we differ as tradesmen break off our connection as friends.
: William Makepeace Thackeray (to his publisher)

Henry James :

EDITH WHARTON mentioned once to Henry James that the car in which she and Henry were riding had been bought with the proceeds of her last novel. "With the proceeds of my last novel," said Henry meditatively, "I purchased a small go-cart, or hand-barrow, on which my guests' luggage is wheeled from the station to my house. It needs a coat of paint. With the proceeds of my next novel I shall have it painted." *: Percy Lubbock*

*Thackeray fought fierce battles
for the rights of authors*

———————————

SOME DAY I hope to write a book, where the royalties will pay for the copies I give away.
: Clarence Darrow

Editorial Headaches: Hazardous Guesses

An editor is a man who knows exactly
what he wants but isn't quite sure.
: *Walter Davenport*

Agonizing choices: An editor at his desk

EDITORS KNOW a lot about things written, but
little about the writing of them. : *Arnold Bennett*

THE CHARACTERISTICS of the good editor-publisher appear to me to be part chameleon, part hummingbird tasting every literary flower, and part warrior-ant. I would emphasize the chameleon aspect because the editor must change his color to reflect changing tastes. Unless he is at all stages of his career the product of the moment, with his eyes on the future, he will succumb to his more alert competitor. : *Cass Canfield*

THERE IS no creative or moral value in the sewage outfall produced by them that have made literature a mere trade; to read such stuff is no real enjoyment; to be addicted to it is a vice; to manufacture it is a crime. : *Frederic Harrison*

AFTER TROLLOPE'S *The Kellys and the O'Kellys* sold no more than 140 copies, his publisher, H. Colburn, wrote to him, "You will perceive it is impossible for us to give any encouragement to you to proceed in novel writing."

DR. JOHNSON may have thought of the editor's function in the writing world when he observed, "A farmer never laid an egg—but he knows more about the process than hens do."

*London street riot on the day
Pope's* Dunciad *was published*

W HEN JOHN MURRAY of London published Byron's *Don Juan* (1819), it caused the kind of sen-
sation that a Hollywood preview of a great motion
picture does today. The crowd in the street clam-
oring for copies was so obstreperous as to neces-
sitate calling the police. *: Cass Canfield*

D URING THE 1920s the incumbent sales manager
of Scribner's was reputed never to have read a
book. When a new Scribner novel came out, he
would take a copy home to his wife. She would
read it over the weekend and the office force would
gather on Monday morning to hear her verdict.
"My wife cried over that book," he would some-
times say, and everybody knew it would be a best-
seller.

But on the Monday after the first bound copies
of F. Scott Fitzgerald's *This Side of Paradise* came
into the office, everybody gathered to hear whether
the sales manager's wife had cried. "That book?
I wouldn't think of showing it to my wife," the
sales manager said. "I picked it up with firetongs
and dropped it into the fire." *: Malcolm Cowley*

Criticizing the Critic

A critic is a man who expects miracles.
: *James G. Huneker*

❧

As FOR YOU, little envious prigs, snarling, bastard, puny criticks, you'll have railed your last; go hang yourselves. : *François Rabelais*

❧

THEY SEIZE upon your publications, as a wrestler seizes upon his opponent's hair, and use them to drag you down, while they themselves remain quite invulnerable, because of their barren pates—so there's nothing for you to get hold of.
: *Sir Thomas More*

❧

No GENIUS was ever blasted by the breath of critics. The poison which, if confined would have burst the heart, fumes away in empty hisses.
: *Samuel Johnson*

❧

EVER SINCE there have been book reviews nobody reads books, except reviewers, and even they do it sloppily. : *Johann Wolfgang von Goethe*

I NEVER READ a book before reviewing it; it prej-
udices a man so. *: Sydney Smith*

I MADE UP my mind: I would have no dealings
with any critic on my own behalf. I would neither
ask for nor deplore criticism, nor would I ever
thank a critic for praise. . . . What can be got by
touting among the critics is never worth the ig-
nominy. *: Anthony Trollope*

*A horde of critics poised to
demolish a book (Woodcut by
Gustave Doré)*

A MAN WHO writes stands up to be shot at.
: *Thomas Hardy*

LISTEN carefully to first criticisms made of your work. Note just what it is about your work that critics don't like—then cultivate it. That's the only part of your work that's individual and worth keeping. : *Jean Cocteau*

READ AS little as possible of literary criticism—such things are either hardened and empty of life or else they are just clever word-games.
: *Rainer Maria Rilke*

IT IS TO BE remembered, and forgiven, that a reviewer, terribly bored by nineteen books out of twenty, is deeply thankful to find the twentieth unboring, and hence he is apt to heap undue laudatory epithets upon it. Such is human nature. And, while authors would never believe it, reviewers are very human. : *Arnold Bennett*

Brief Critiques

MY DEAR Sir,
I have read your play. Oh, my Dear Sir!
: Sir Herbert Beerbohm Tree

⁌

THIS NOVEL is not to be tossed lightly aside, but
to be hurled with great force. *: Dorothy Parker*

⁌

REVIEW OF a critic after seeing Christopher Ish-
erwood's *I Am a Camera:* "No Leica."

⁌

Critics attack a book

The Retail End: Bookshops, Antiquarians, Auctioneers

Where is human nature so weak
as in a bookstore?

: Henry Ward Beecher

❧

IGNORANT ASSES visiting stationers' shops, their use is not to inquire for good books, but new books. *: John Webster*

❧

LORD! WHEN you sell a man a book you don't sell just twelve ounces of paper and ink and glue—you sell him a whole new life. Love and friendship and humour and ships at sea by night—there's all heaven and earth in a book, a real book. *: Christopher Morley*

❧

A seventeenth-century bookstall in the Palais Royal, Paris

A PUBLISHER must accustom the public to the spectacle of many books. If a bookshop displayed only the few really good books that get published in a year, it would be nearly empty. It would not attract. The public would not enter it. The bookseller would expire, and his family would go on the dole. *: Arnold Bennett*

*Samuel Johnson's first job when
coming to London was in Osborne's bookshop.
When reprimanded by Osborne for browsing,
Johnson, enraged, knocked the bookseller down.*

⁂

SOME GOOD books won't sell, no matter what
you do, other good books won't stop selling no
matter what you do or don't do. *: Peter Schwed*

⁂

THE STUDENT, when he enters one of the great
bookshops in his university town, is learning the
extremely important part of educating himself.
Browsing in a bookshop teaches him to explore
the wide world of literature, and to do this on his
own initiative without guidance. He is learning to
find his way for himself and finding his way for
himself is one of the most important parts of education. *: Arnold Toynbee*

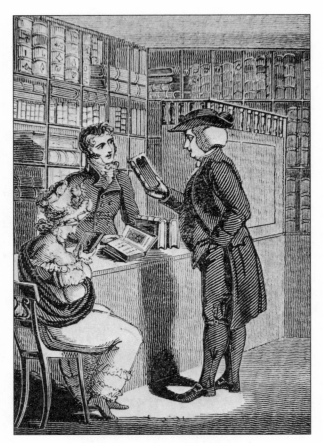

Bibliophile examines leatherbound
treasures in a London bookshop

Aᴛᴛᴇɴᴅɪɴɢ ʙᴏᴏᴋ auctions is (for the book-
lover) the greatest, the most stirring of adventures.
The lust of books is here seen at its heights: faces
that are usually poker portraits become sharply
distorted, eyes which ordinarily indulge an almost
studied innocence shoot sudden darts of fire.
: A. S. W. Rosenbach

Book *Banners*

Are we to have a censor whose
imprimatur shall say what books may be
sold, and what we may buy?
: *Thomas Jefferson*

.:.

A WISE MAN, like a good refiner, can gather gold
out of the drossiest volume, and a fool will be a
fool with the best book, yea, or without a book.
There is no reason that we should deprive a wise
man of any advantage to his wisdom, while we
seek to restrain from a fool that which being re-
trained will be no hindrance to his folly.
: *John Milton*

.:.

GIVE ME six lines written by the most honorable
of men and I will find an excuse in them to hang
him. : *Cardinal Richelieu*

.:.

I THANK GOD that we have no free schools nor
printing. And I hope we shall not have these in
three hundred years. For learning has brought dis-
obedience and heresy and sects into the world,
and printing has divulged them and libels against
the government. : *Sir William Berkeley*

To LIMIT the press is to insult a nation; to prohibit reading of certain books is to declare the inhabitants to be either fools or slaves.
: *Claude-Adrien Helvétius*

WHY SHOULD freedom of speech and freedom of the press be allowed? Why should a government which is doing what it believes to be right allow itself to be criticized? It would not allow opposition by lethal weapons. Ideas are much more fatal things than guns. Why should any man be allowed to buy a printing press and disseminate pernicious opinions calculated to embarrass the government?
: *Vladimir Ilyich Lenin*

GOD FORBID that any book should be banned. The practice is as indefensible as infanticide.
: *Rebecca West*

BEING ONE of Nature's non-censors, I simply cannot understand why any human being should want to prevent other responsible human beings from writing or reading what they like.
: *Aldous Huxley*

Dodging the bookbanners: Publishing on the run.
To escape censors, French printers
issued pamphlets via "itinerant printshops."

To choose a good book, look in an inquisitor's prohibited list. : *John Aikin*

There is a distinct affinity between fools and censorship. It seems to be one of those breeding grounds where they rush in.
: *Heywood Campbell Broun*

Books won't stay banned—Ideas won't go to jail. : *Alfred Whitney Griswold*

Every human being has a right to hear what other wise human beings have spoken to him. It is one of the Rights of Men; a very cruel injustice if you deny it to a man! : *Thomas Carlyle*

Book Burners

The paper burns, but the words fly away.
: *Akiba ben Joseph*
(last words at the stake when the Torah also was being burned)

King decrees destruction of the works of St. Jerome
(Woodcut 1523)

WHERE BOOKS are burned, human beings will
in the end be burned too. : *Heinrich Heine*

B<small>OOKS</small>—they have been beaten and burned, drowned, tortured, imprisoned, suppressed, executed, exiled, reviled, condemned, buried.
: *Holbrook Jackson*

W<small>HO KILLS</small> a man kills a reasonable creature, God's image; but he who destroys a good book kills reason itself, kills the image of God, as it were; he slays an immortality rather than a life.
: *John Milton*

A <small>CERTAIN</small> Goth when his countrymen came into Greece, and would have burned all their books, he cried out against it . . . by all means they shouldn't do it; "Leave them that plague which in time will consume all their vigor, and martial spirit."
: *Robert Burton*

W<small>E ALL KNOW</small> that books burn, yet we have the greater knowledge that books cannot be killed by fire. People die, but books never die. . . . Books are weapons . . . make them weapons for man's freedom. : *Franklin D. Roosevelt*

Books set afire in the Alexandrian Library
(From World Chronicle 1493)

EVERY BURNED book enlightens the world.
: *Ralph Waldo Emerson*

*Benjamin Franklin, the colonies' premier
bookman, welcomes goddess of freedom*

PART FOUR

The Book in America: Freedom to Think, to Write, to be Informed

A Nation of Readers

I conceive that a knowledge of books is
the basis on which all other knowledge rests.
: George Washington

❖

Knowledge and entertainment in the portable
form of books came to America with its first col-
onist, and reading for profit or pleasure has ever
since been an integral part of the life of this
land. . . . Boston in 1640, which had not yet got
around to naming its streets, had far more than a
normal share of bookstores. The New Englanders
frequently spent an evening by the light of the
chimney-fire reading Foxe's *Book of Martyres,* that
dramatic account of Protestant sufferings.
: James D. Hart

❖

Lady offers literary ware from her
rolling bookstore (Woodcut by
Gorskin in Christopher Morley's
Parnassus on Wheels)

Benjamin Franklin:

"From a child . . . all the little money that came into my hands was ever laid out on books."

Franklin reminisced that when young he often read all through the night

FRANKLIN, after chartering the first subscription library in Philadelphia in 1731, noted in his autobiography the spread of reading among his contemporaries: "Reading became more fashionable and our People having no public Amusements to divert their Attention from Study became better acquainted with Books, and in a few Years were observ'd by Strangers to be better instructed and more intelligent than People of the same Rank generally are in other Countries."

THOUGH FRANKLIN in his earliest years read as a tradesman in a way that was "snug and gave no scandal" he was actually an avid and powerful reader of books. There were always books in his inner life, books in his business, books in his friendships. : *Mark Van Doren*

A
CATALOGUE
OF
CHOICE AND VALUABLE
BOOKS,
CONSISTING OF

Near 600 Volumes, in most Faculties and Sciences, *viz.*

DIVINITY, HISTORY, LAW, MA-
THEMATICS, PHILOSOPHY, PHY-
SIC, POETRY, &c.

Which will begin
TO BE SOLD for Ready Money only, by BENJ.
FRANKLIN; at the *Post-Office* in *Philadelphia*,
on Wednesday, the 11th of *April* 1744. at Nine
a Clock in the Morning ; And, for Dispatch, the
lowest Price is mark'd in each Book.
The Sale to continue Three Weeks, and no longer ;
and what then remains will be sold at an advanced
Price.

Those Persons that live remote, by sending their
Orders and Money to said B. FRANKLIN, may
depend on the same Justice as if present.

Franklin poster announcing book sale
"for ready cash," April 1744

Tom Paine's Pamphlets:
A Clarion Call to Independence

~~~~~~~~~~~~~~~~~~~~~~~~~~~~~~~~~~~

The American cause owed as much to the pen of Paine as to the sword of Washington.

∴

PAINE, "the rebellious staymaker," had arrived in America in 1774, a self-educated and penniless Quaker. He wrote *Common Sense* after the battle of Lexington to prove that independence and a republican government were feasible. His stirring tract, *The Crisis,* was written by firelight while serving under General Washington. Looking back, Paine reflected, "It was the cause of America that made me an author." *: Bernard Smith*

∵

COMMON SENSE sold 100,000 copies in ten weeks. No other book had gained such quick and widespread distribution. One copy was sold for every twenty-five people in the colonies—men, women and children, Whigs and Tories alike. Relative to the population no other book had such a widespread distribution. *: James D. Hart*

∴

*"Mad" Tom Paine wrote his pamphlets
to vanquish British rule in America*

COMMON SENSE:

ADDRESSED TO THE

INHABITANTS

OF

A M E R I C A.

On the following interesting

S U B J E C T S.

I. Of the Origin and Design of Government in general, with concise Remarks on the English Constitution.

II. Of Monarchy and Hereditary Succession.

III. Thoughts on the present State of American Affairs.

IV. Of the present Ability of America, with some miscellaneous Reflections.

Written by an ENGLISHMAN.

By Thomas Paine

Man knows no Master save creating HEAVEN,
Or those whom choice and common good ordain.
THOMSON.

PHILADELPHIA, Printed
And Sold by R. BELL, in Third-Street, 1776.

Title page to Common Sense *which became immediate bestseller*

·❖·

HAVE YOU seen the pamphlet *Common Sense*? I never saw such a masterly, irresistable performance. . . . It will, if I mistake not . . . give the "coup de grace" to Great Britain.
: General Henry Lee to George Washington

❖

The Nation Established: Reading Expands, Learning Flourishes

THE REVOLUTION won, intellectual activities were opened to all, for a republican government demanded a literate and enlightened public. As one magazine contributor put it: "From public schools shall general knowledge flow, For it's the public's right-to-know." : *James D. Hart*

SINCE THE eighteen-twenties Boston had tingled with a new ambition. . . . Learning was endemic in a town whose first inhabitant, the Cambridge scholar Braxton, had brought his library with him. There had been books on the slope of Beacon Hill when the wolves still howled on the summit. : *Van Wyck Brooks*

LEARNING WAS keenly pursued, omnipresent at Harvard. The shopkeepers around Harvard Square added tags of Latin to their signs. The janitor of the newly established law school was a notable spouter of Virgil. : *Van Wyck Brooks*

The establishment of schools to lay the foundations for responsible citizenship was considered a prime task in communities of the young republic

Noah Webster: "The Schoolmaster of the Republic."
His best-selling speller and dictionaries
made his name an eponym of world-renown.
He inspired the citizens of the new nation to read.

Three Pioneer American Bookmen

❧

NOAH WEBSTER

Linguist, Champion of Copyright, Bookdealer

THIS SON of a New England farmer had hob-nobbed with Washington and Franklin, pamphle-teered for the adoption of the Constitution, gained renown as a lecturer on the English language . . . and hustled his own books tirelessly.
: *Van Wyck Brooks*

❧

NOAH WEBSTER, the pioneer in many fields of endeavor on the American frontier, taught the masses to spell and read. He was truly the school-master of the Republic . . . His *Spelling Book* played a fundamental part in American education. It was so widely used that by 1890, sixty million copies had been sold. To protect his linguistic ef-fort, Webster became an early champion of copy-right protection. His aim: "to see America as independent and illustrious in letters as it is al-ready in civil policy." : *Erwin C. Shoemaker*

ELIHU BURRITT
Voracious Reader, Visionary Pacifist

Born in 1810 in the Yankee village of New Britain, Connecticut, Elihu Burritt was the third in a struggling family of ten children. The emphasis on "self culture" caused him to elevate himself from a poor untutored blacksmith to a lyceum lecturer and peace advocate of international repute. Though apprenticed to a laboring trade as a young boy, Elihu stubbornly pursued his love of books and learning. "I carried my indomitable taste for reading to the blacksmith shop," he related, "and studied Greek while blowing the bellows."
: *Merle Curti*

MASON LOCKE WEEMS
"The Book Peddling Parson"

Humanity and Patriotism both cry aloud for Books, Books, Books. : *Parson Weems*

The reverend Parson Weems lives on in American history . . . as the person who supposedly made up the story of young George Washington and the cherry tree. . . . He entered that tale into his little book about Washington that in one edition or another has outsold every other book about Washington ever written. . . . Parson Weems endures, a ghost figure on the outskirts of our national literature. : *Lewis Leary*

Elihu Burritt studying Greek while
working as a blacksmith on the road
during one of his trips promoting world peace

*The cherry tree legend first appeared
in Weems's best-selling Washington
biography, becoming a part of
American folklore*

THE SIGHT of Parson Weems, with his cart packed with books for sale, was a familiar one along the dirt roads and byways of the early United States. Weems undertook to bring books and culture to the towns, cities, farms, and plantations along the Atlantic coast and well into the interior . . . After a day on the road, Parson Weems sharpened his quill and let his fancy roam in the realm of history and hero worship. He had prepared his biography of Washington fortuitously in the summer of 1799. When Washington died on December 14 of that year the demand for Weems's 25 cent book skyrocketed. "Millions are gasping to read something about him. The people are tearing me to pieces . . . I can sell 10,000 copies in Virginia alone." *: Van Wyck Brooks*

The Book That Roused the Nation

God wrote it . . . I took his dictation.
: *Harriet Beecher Stowe*

᠅

Hᴀʀʀɪᴇᴛ ʙᴇᴇᴄʜᴇʀ Stowe's *Uncle Tom's Cabin* ran first in ten monthly installments in the *National Era*. It was published in ten months and she received only $300 as a fee. Finally, when *Uncle Tom's Cabin* came out in book form, the Stowes hoped that Harriet might "get a new silk dress out of it." It made her the richest author in America—though she was to squander her wealth.
: *Edward Wagenknecht*

᠅

Wʜᴇɴ *Uncle Tom's Cabin* arrived in England in the spring of 1852, twenty-seven editions were quickly sold; more than a million copies by the end of the year. Mrs. Stowe sent copies to Prince Albert, Lord Shaftesbury, and other prominent English people known to be interested in the slavery question. The Queen read the book and was much moved by it. During her first public appearance in London Mrs. Stowe's huge audience stood until she sat down, an honor ordinarily reserved for the Queen. : *Amy Cruse*

UNCLE TOM'S Cabin achieved the greatest sales and the greatest social influence of any novel of this epic age . . . it set a standard for women writers. It was women, the mothers of America on whom Mrs. Stowe placed responsibility for the abolition of slavery. : *Ellen Moers*

I SINCERELY veil my face before a mighty subject as that handled in Mrs. Stowe's work.
: *Charlotte Brontë*

THOUGH LINCOLN engaged in permissible hyperbole when he said that it was "the book by the little lady that made the big war,"—there is no doubt that *Uncle Tom's Cabin* incited worldwide public awareness of the curse of slavery and marked the most powerful appeal to have it wiped out. Hence it was a book—as Victor Hugo had observed in our first quote—that marked the transition from "man-slave to free-man."

Harriet Beecher Stowe: In Lincoln's words, "the little woman who made the big war." Uncle Tom's Cabin made America and the world aware of slavery's injustice and inhumanity, paving the way for slave-man to become free-man.

135,000 SETS, 270,000 VOLUMES SOLD.

UNCLE TOM'S CABIN

FOR SALE HERE.

AN EDITION FOR THE MILLION, COMPLETE IN 1 Vol., PRICE 37 1-2 CENTS.
" " IN GERMAN, IN 1 Vol., PRICE 50 CENTS.
" " IN 2 Vols., CLOTH, 6 PLATES, PRICE $1.50.
SUPERB ILLUSTRATED EDITION, IN 1 Vol., WITH 153 ENGRAVINGS,
PRICES FROM $2.50 TO $5.00.

The Greatest Book of the Age.

The book that roused the world
to free the slaves from bondage

The Center for the Book

Established by law in 1977 at the urging of Librarian of Congress Daniel J. Boorstin, the Center for the Book in the Library of Congress has two purposes: to stimulate public interest in books and reading and to encourage the study of books and their role in society. Its activities include reading promotion projects such as Read More About It and Books Make a Difference, symposia, lectures, exhibitions, and, of course, the publication of books. Over 50 books and pamphlets have been published for general and scholarly audiences, including *The Book* by Barbara Tuchman, *Born to Trouble: One Hundred Years of Huckleberry Finn,* by Justin Kaplan, *Fine Printing: The San Francisco Tradition,* by James D. Hart, and *Literacy in Historical Perspective,* edited by Daniel P. Resnick.

An encouraging development in the Center for the Book's efforts "to keep the book flourishing" has been the creation, since 1984, of 11 state or regional affiliates of the Center. The first was the Florida Center for the Book, which is located at the Broward County Library in Fort Lauderdale. Its innovative projects have included the establishment of a literary landmark honoring Florida author John D. MacDonald and his fictional character Travis McGee and development of a "Books Aboard" burgee or pennant, to be flown by boats when book lovers are aboard. The other affiliated centers are California, Illinois, Iowa, Michigan, Oklahoma, Oregon, Texas, Upper Midwest (Minnesota, North Dakota, South Dakota), Virginia, and Wisconsin.

All of the Center for the Book's projects and the activities of its 11 affiliates are supported by private, tax deductible contributions from individuals, corporations, and foundations. For further information, write the Center for the Book, Library of Congress, Washingon, D.C. 20540.

JOHN Y. COLE
Director, The Center for the Book

The Library of Congress

A C K N O W L E D G M E N T S

❖

Grateful acknowledgment is made to the following publishers and authors for permission to use copyrighted material:

Algonquin Books of Chapel Hill: Extract from *The Book-Peddling Parson* by Lewis Leary, copyright 1984 by Lewis Leary. Reprinted by permission of the publisher.

American Heritage: Extract from "Extraordinary Lives" edited by William Zinsser, copyright 1985. Reprinted by permission of the publisher.

Enid Bagnold: Extract from *Enid Bagnold's Autobiography,* copyright 1969 by Enid Bagnold. Reprinted by permission of the Estate of Enid Bagnold.

Jacques Barzun: Extract from On *Writing, Editing & Publishing* by Jacques Barzun. Chicago: University of Chicago Press, 1971. Reprinted by permission of the author.

Norman Cousins: From *World Magazine,* copyright 1952. Reprinted by permission of the author.

Malcolm Cowley: From *The New Yorker,* copyright 1944. Renewal copyright 1972 by Malcolm Cowley. Reprinted by permission of the author.

E. P. Dutton, Inc.: Extract from *The World of Washington Irving* by Van Wyck Brooks, copyright 1946. Reprinted by permission of the publisher.

Faber & Faber, Inc.: Extract from *The Real Thing* by Tom Stoppard, copyright 1984 by Tom Stoppard. Reprinted by permission of the publisher.

Farrar, Straus and Giroux, Inc.: Extract from *Reading Myself And Others* by Philip Roth. Copyright © 1961, 1963, 1969, 1970, 1971, 1972, 1973, 1974, 1975 by Philip Roth. Reprinted by permission of Farrar, Straus and Giroux, Inc.

The quotes in this book have been collected over many years. At times, in the excitement of the chase, I may not have taken the time required for complete authentication. If any holders of rights have been inadvertently overlooked, I offer my apologies and the promise of correction in subsequent printings.

O.L.B.

PICTURE CREDITS

Aiken, John (1747–1822)
English physician and author.

Akiba ben Joseph (c.50–c.135 A.D.)
Jewish rabbi and martyr.

Aquinas, Saint Thomas (1225–1274)
Italian philosopher and theologian.

Aristotle (384–322 B.C.)
Greek philosopher.

Ascham, Roger (1515–1568)
English humanist and scholar.

Babel, Isaac (1894–1941)
Russian writer and playwright.

Bagnold, Enid (1889–1981)
English novelist and playwright.

Baldwin, James (b. 1924)
American writer.

Balfour, Lord Arthur (1848–1930)
English philosopher and statesman.

Barzun, Jacques (b. 1907)
American writer and educator.

Baudelaire, Charles (1821–1867)
French poet and critic.

Beecher, Henry Ward (1813–1887)
American clergyman.

Belloc, Hilaire (1870–1953)
English author.

Ben-Gurion, David (1886–1973)
Israeli statesman.

Benchley, Robert (1889–1945)
American humorist.

Benét, Stephen Vincent (1898–1943)
American poet.

Bennet, Arnold (1867–1931)
English novelist and dramatist.

Berkeley, Sir William (1601–1677)
Colonial governor of Virginia.

Berman, Jeffrey (b. 1945)
American writer.

Boorstin, Daniel J. (b. 1914)
Librarian of Congress, historian.

Boswell, James (1740–1795)
Scottish author.

Brontë, Charlotte (1816–1855)
English novelist.

Brooks, Van Wyck (1886–1963)
American literary historian.

Broun, Heywood Campbell (1888–1939)
American columnist and critic.

Brown, John Mason (1900–1969)
American literary critic.

Burton, Robert (1577–1640)
English clergyman and author.

Burrit, Elihu (1810–1879)
American reformer and linguist.

Bury, Richard de (1287–1345)
English ecclesiastic and book collector.

Butler, Samuel (1835–1902)
English author.

Byron, Lord George Gordon (1788–1824)
English poet.

Calvino, Italo (1923–1985)
Italian novelist

Canfield, Cass (1897–1985)
American publisher.

Carlyle, Thomas (1795–1881)
Scottish historian and essayist.

Carroll, Lewis (1832–1898)
(Charles Dodgson) English writer.

Cather, Willa (1876–1947)
American novelist.

Cerf, Bennett (1898–1972)
American publisher.

Channing, William Ellery (1780–1842)
American minister and author.

Chappell, Warren (b. 1904)
American book designer.

Chesterfield, Lord Philip (1694–1773)
English statesman and author.

Chesterton, G. K. (1874–1936)
English journalist.

Churchill, Sir Winston (1874–1965)
English statesman and author.

Chute, Marchette (b. 1909)
American writer.

Cicero, Marcus Tullius (106–43 B.C.)
Roman orator.

Cocteau, Jean (1889–1963)
French poet, filmmaker and writer.

Colton, Charles Caleb (1630–1687)
English poet.

Conger, Lesley (b. 1922)
American writer.

Connolly, Cyril (1903–1974)
English essayist, critic and editor.

Conrad, Joseph (1857–1924)
English novelist.

Cousins, Norman (b. 1912)
American writer and editor.

Cowley, Abraham (1618–1667)
English poet.

Cowley, Malcolm (b. 1898)
American editor and writer.

Crane, Hart (1899–1932)
American poet.

Cruse, Amy (1870–19?)
British writer.

Curti, Merle (b. 1897)
American historian.

Darrow, Clarence (1857–1938)
American lawyer.

Davenport, Walter (1889–1971)
American writer.

Dewey, Melvil (1851–1931)
American librarian.

Dickens, Charles (1812–1870)
English novelist.

Dickinson, Emily (1830-1886)
American poet.

Disraeli, Lord Benjamin (1804–1881)
English statesman.

D'Israeli, Isaac (1766–1848)
English literary historian.

Duhamel, Georges (1884–1966)
French novelist and playwright.

Edel, Leon (b. 1907)
American critic and biographer.

Eliot, George (1819–1880)
(Mary Ann Evans) English novelist.

Eliot, T. S. (1888–1965)
English poet and critic.

Elizabeth I (1533–1603)
Queen of England.

Emerson, Ralph Waldo (1803–1882)
American essayist and poet.

Faulkner, William (1897–1962)
American novelist.

Field, Eugene (1850–1895)
American poet and writer.

Fitzgerald, F. Scott (1896–1940)
American novelist.

Flaubert, Gustave (1821–1880)
French novelist.

Forster, E. M. (1879–1970)
English novelist and critic.

France, Anatole (1844–1924)
(Jacques Thibault) French novelist.

Franklin, Benjamin (1706–1790)
American statesman.

Freud, Sigmund (1856–1939)
Founder of psychoanalysis.

George II (1683–1760)
King of England.

Gladstone, William Ewart (1809–1898)
English statesman.

Glasgow, Ellen (1873–1945)
American novelist.

Goethe, Johann Wolfgang von (1747–1832)
German poet.

Griswold, Alfred Whitney (b. 1906)
American educator.

Guiterman, Arthur (1871–1943)
American satirist.

Hardwick, Elizabeth (b. 1916)
American essayist.

Hardy, Thomas (1840–1928)
English novelist.

Hare, Augustus (1792–1834)
English clergyman and essayist.

Harrison, Frederic (1831–1923)
English jurist and writer.

Hart, James D. (b. 1911)
American literary historian.

Hart-Davis, Rupert (b. 1907)
English publisher.

Hay, Denys (b. 1915)
English historian.

Heine, Heinrich (1797–1856)
German lyric poet.

Helvétius, Claude Adrien (1715–1771)
French philosopher.

Hemingway, Ernest (1899–1961)
American writer.

Hogg, Thomas Jefferson (1792–1862)
English biographer.

Holmes, Oliver Wendell (1802–1894)
American author and physician.

Hooker, Richard (1554?–1600)
English theologian.

Houser, M. L. (1871–1951)
American writer.

Hubbard, Elbert (1856–1915)
American author and publisher.

Hubbard, Frank McKinney (1868–1930)
American humorist.

Hughes, Rupert (1872–1956)
American writer.

Hugo, Victor (1802–1885)
French novelist, poet and playwright.

Huneker, James G. (1860–1921)
American essayist and music critic.

Huxley, Aldous (1894–1963)
English novelist.

Irving, Washington (1783–1859)
American writer.

Jackson, Holbrook (1874–1948)
English writer.

James I (1566–1625)
King of England.

James, Henry (1843–1916)
American novelist and critic.

Jefferson, Thomas (1743–1826)
3d president of the United States.

Johnson, Samuel (1709–1784)
English critic.

Jones, James (1921–1971)
American writer.

Jong, Erica (b. 1942)
American novelist and poet.

Kafka, Franz (1883–1924)
Austrian writer.

Kazin, Alfred (b. 1915)
American critic.

Keats, John (1795–1821)
English poet.

Kilpatrick, James (b. 1920)
American journalist.

King, William (1663–1712)
English satirist.

Lamb, Charles (1775–1834)
English essayist.

Larkin, Philip (1922–1985)
English poet.

Lawrence, D. H. (1885–1930)
English novelist.

Leary, Lewis (b. 1906)
American writer.

Lenin, Vladimir Ilyich (1870–1924)
Russian Communist leader.

Lichtenberg, George C. (1742–1799)
German satirist and physicist.

Lincoln, Abraham (1809–1865)
16th president of the United States.

Locke, John (1632–1704)
English philosopher.

Longfellow, Henry Wadsworth (1807–1882)
American poet.

Lowell, James Russell (1819–1891)
American poet, critic and editor.

Lower, Sam (1797–1868)
English writer.

Lubbock, Percy (1879–1965)
English essayist.

Ludwig, Emil (1881–1943)
German biographer.

McCarthy, Mary (b. 1912)
American writer.

McCullough, David (b. 1933)
American biographer.

MacLeish, Archibald (1892–1982)
American poet, Librarian of Congress.

Mallarmé, Stéphane (1842–1898)
French poet.

McLuhan, Marshall (1911–1980)
Canadian communication theorist.

Marquis, Don (1878–1937)
American journalist and poet.

Marvell, Andrew (1621–1678)
English poet.

Maugham, W. Somerset (1874–1965)
English novelist.

Maurois, André (1885–1967)
French biographer.

Melville, Herman (1819–1891)
American novelist.

Mencken, H. L. (1880–1956)
American editor and satirist.

Meredith, George (1828–1909)
English novelist and poet.

Miller, Henry (1891–1980)
American author.

Milton, John (1609–1674)
English poet.

Moers, Ellen (1928–1979)
American literary historian.

Montagu, Lady Mary Wortley (1689–1762)
English epistolarian.

Montaigne, Michel de (1553–1592)
French essayist.

More, Sir Thomas (1478–1535)
English statesman.

Morley, Christopher (1890–1957)
American writer and editor.

Münsterberg, Hugo (1863–1916)
American psychologist.

Napoleon I (1769–1821)
Emperor of France.

Newton, Alfred Edward (1863–1940)
American bibliophile.

Nietzsche, Friedrich (1844–1900)
German philosopher.

O'Connell, Daniel (1775–1847)
Irish political leader.

Orwell, George (1903–1950)
(Eric Blair) English novelist, essayist.

Oswald, John Clyde (1872–1938)
American biographer and printer.

Paine, Thomas (1737–1809)
Revolutionary pamphleteer.

Parker, Dorothy (1893–1967)
American satirist.

Pascal, Blaise (1623–1662)
French philosopher.

Pater, Walter (1839–1894)
English essayist.

Petrarca, Francesco (1304–1374)
Italian poet.

Poe, Edgar Allan (1809–1849)
American poet and critic.

Pope, Alexander (1688–1744)
English poet.

Pound, Ezra (1885–1972)
American poet, critic and editor.

Powell, Lawrence C. (b. 1906)
American librarian.

Proust, Marcel (1871–1922)
French novelist.

Rabelais, François (c.1490–1553)
French satirist and physician.

Ray, John (1627–1705)
English naturalist.

Richelieu, Cardinal (1585–1642)
French statesman.

Rilke, Rainer Maria (1875–1926)
German lyric poet.

Roosevelt, Franklin Delano (1882–1945)
32nd president of the United States.

Rosenbach, A. S. W. (1876–1952)
American bibliophile.

Rosten, Leo (b. 1908)
American humorist and writer.

Roth, Philip (b. 1933)
American novelist.

Russell, John (b. 1919)
American art historian and critic.

Sagan, Françoise (b. 1935)
(Françoise Quoirez) French writer.

Sainte-Beuve, Charles A. (1804–1869)
French literary historian and critic.

Sayers, Frances Clarke (b. 1897)
American librarian.

Schoenberg, Arnold (1874–1951)
Austrian composer.

Schopenhauer, Arthur (1788–1860)
German philosopher.

Schwed, Peter (b. 1911)
American publisher.

Scott, Sir Walter (1771–1832)
Scottish novelist.

Sévigné, Marquise Marie de (1626–1696)
French epistolarian.

Shakespeare, William (1564–1616)
English dramatist and poet.

Shaw, George Bernard (1856–1950)
Irish playwright and writer.

Shelley, Percy Bysshe (1792–1822)
English poet.

Sheridan, Richard Brinsley (1751–1816)
Irish dramatist.

Simon, Claude (b. 1911)
French novelist.

Sitwell, Sir Osbert (1892–1969)
English poet and writer.

Smith, Alexander (1830–1867)
Scottish poet.

Smith, Bernard (b. 1906)
American historian.

Smith, Logan Pearsall (1865–1946)
Anglo-American author.

Smith, Sydney (1771–1845)
English clergyman and writer.

Socrates (469–399 B.C.)
Greek philosopher.

Steinbeck, John (1902–1968)
American novelist.

Steinem, Gloria (b. 1936)
American writer.

Steiner, George (b. 1929)
American critic.

Stern, Philip Van Doren (b. 1900)
American biographer.

Stevenson, Robert Louis (1850–1894)
Scottish novelist, poet and essayist.

Stoppard, Tom (b. 1937)
English dramatist.

Stowe, Harriet Beecher (1811–1896)
American writer.

Strachey, Lytton (1880–1932)
English biographer and critic.

Styron, William (b. 1925)
American novelist.

Swift, Jonathan (1667–1745)
English satirist.

Thackeray, William Makepeace (1811–1863)
English novelist.

Thomas, Alan G. (b. 1906)
English bookdealer.

Thoreau, Henry David (1817–1862)
American writer and naturalist.

Tolstoy, Count Leo (1828–1910)
Russian novelist.

Toynbee, Arnold (1889–1975)
English historian.

Tree, Sir Herbert Beerbohm (1853–1917)
English actor-manager.

Trollope, Anthony (1815–1882)
English novelist.

Tuchman, Barbara W. (b. 1912)
American historian.

Twain, Mark (1835–1910)
(Samuel Clemens) American humorist.

Unseld, Siegfried (b. 1924)
German publisher

Updike, John (b. 1932)
American novelist and critic.

Uzanne, Octave (1852–1931)
French bibliophile.

Valéry, Paul (1871–1945)
French poet and critic.

Van Doren, Mark (1894–1973)
American critic.

Voltaire (1694–1778)
(François-Marie Arouet) French writer.

Vorse, Mary Heaton (1874–1966)
American writer.

Wagenknecht, Edward (b. 1900)
American writer.

Walpole, Sir Hugh (1884–1941)
English novelist.

Walpole, Sir Robert (1676–1745)
English statesman.

Washington, George (1732–1799)
1st president of the United States.

Webster, John (1580?–1634)
English playwright.

Webster, Noah (1758–1843)
American lexicographer.

Weems, Mason Locke (1759–1859)
American author and preacher.

Weidman, Jerome (b. 1913)
American novelist.

Weldon, Fay (b. 1933)
English novelist.

West, Dame Rebecca (1892–1983)
English novelist.

White, E. B. (1899–1985)
American essayist.

Wolfe, Thomas (1900–1938)
American writer.

Woolf, Virginia (1882–1941)
English novelist and essayist.

THE DELIGHTS OF READING

has been set by NK Graphics, Keene, New Hampshire, in Times Roman, a typeface designed by Stanley Morison for the London *Times*. The basic design objective of maximum legibility in minimum space has resulted in the larger letter structure that makes each point size seem the equivalent of a size larger in most other types.

The book has been printed and bound by Maple-Vail Book Manufacturing Group, Binghamton, New York. Designed by Designworks, Inc.